WOMEN AND CREATIVITY

DOLORES R. LECKEY

1991 Madeleva Lecture
in Spirituality

PAULIST PRESS
New York/Mahwah

Library of Congress Cataloging-in-Publication Data

Leckey, Dolores R.
    Women and creativity: 1991 Madeleva lecture in spirituality / by Dolores R. Leckey
      p. cm.
    Includes bibliographical references.
    ISBN 0-8091-3259-1
    1. Women, Catholic—Religious life. 2. Women–Psychology. 3. Christian communities—Catholic Church. 4. Creative ability—Religious aspects—Christianity. 5. Church work with women—Catholic Church. 6. Catholic Church—History—1965-   I. Title. II. Title: Madeleva lecture in spirituality.
BX2347.8.W6L42   1991
282'.082—dc20
                              90-26700
                               CIP

Published by Paulist Press
997 Macarthur Blvd.
Mahwah, N.J. 07430

Printed and bound in the United States of America

TABLE OF CONTENTS

To Sister Edith Petrone, O.P.
teacher, friend, believer
in women's creativity.

***

Dolores Leckey is the executive director of the Secretariat for Laity and Family Life of the National Conference of Catholic Bishops. This Secretariat serves three bishops' committees: Marriage and Family, Laity, and Women in Society and in the Church. It also is the lead agent for Catholic Conference youth programs. Dolores Leckey has been a teacher, a public television producer and a retreat leader. The author of several books and numerous articles, she lectures widely in the United States and abroad. She has served as an advisor to the U.S. bishops' delegations to both the 1980 and 1987 Roman synods. The recipient of six honorary doctorates and Washington Theological Union's Distinguished Service Award (1988), she is a wife, mother, grandmother and civic activist committed to affordable housing in local communities.

INTRODUCTION

How can we discover what is truly valuable in another's life? What does she prize? What is essential to integrity? One window of insight is the person's available writings. Essays, fiction, journals and memoirs, poems, autobiography, all admit light into a person's interior spaces. Identifying other writers whom one respects is another window. Czeslaw Milosz, for example, the Polish Nobel Prize winning poet, has published a collection of poetry and prose by a variety of authors, together with fragments of his own work, to form a kind of collage of what he believes to be the shaping forces of his own life and art.[1] We know more about Milosz because of his disclosures and analyses.

Not everyone is so organized and direct about laying out the golden threads followed in the course of spiritual and intellectual ascent. Sometimes clues are scattered in the halls and stairways of one's life. Sister Madeleva, for whom this lecture series is named, was such a one. Over and above the major theme of her poetic work—the soul's love affair with God—one discovers other themes, subplots as it were, of how she viewed life and literature. Her elegant essays are an important source of these discoveries.

We learn, for example, that Sr. Madeleva admired

the work of Edna St. Vincent Millay, and not simply for Millay's control of thought and feeling, but also for the social thrust of Millay's writing. Quoting Carl Van Doren who said of Millay that, "She reveals women as they are not as they are supposed to be"[2] one senses that Sr. Madeleva, too, valued that kind of creative courage, a courage that opens the way to "the discovering of new forms, new symbols, new patterns on which a new society can be built."[3] And while Sr. Madeleva intimates that the world was not quite ready to receive Millay's service of rendering her truth about women, I think a readiness is evident today.

All the institutions of society have been affected to some degree by the women's movement. Law, medicine, business, government, marriage and family, the church —these institutions are different today than they were in the early years of this century when both Edna St. Vincent Millay and Sister Madeleva were writing; and they are different, to some degree at least, because of the presence of women, in a new way, within these institutions. The new presence is that of co-equal partnership and leadership which allows the telling of how women really are, (and how they really were) in their homes, in their workplaces, in the solitude of their souls, not how they are supposed to be. The growing public discourse by and about women, to which the Madeleva lectures contribute, helps to tell the true story of women. Like Millay's work, the Madeleva lectures speak of women's reality. Women at prayer, scripture as a key to understanding women's spirituality, women's passion for God, women and power—these and other topics have been explored in these lectures. This year I want to consider the creativity of women, especially from the perspective of Christian culture. Is there a uniqueness to women's creativity? If so, what is it? And what hope does it offer to the church and to the world?

This interest in the question of women and creativity has been with me my entire adult life, but in the last decade the question has gathered momentum. Several years ago I was introduced to the poetry of Jessica Powers, a poet who lived for forty-seven years the life of a cloistered Carmelite. As a promising poet who lived in Wisconsin and in New York City during the 1930s she chose the rigors of Carmel (entering in 1941) over the stimulus of literary salons. Why, I wondered. I thought about a friend, a widow who is the mother of ten children who in her fifties embarked on a new career as a poetry therapist, and who in her sixties became a Benedictine nun. Here were two women with considerable capacities for explicit creative expression and who had chosen for themselves a most structured way of being in life, one with boundaries and routines, rituals and limits. If creativity requires a kind of disobedience to normality, as Loren Eiseley says,[4] then perhaps convent life offered a counter-normality, a structure that allowed women to move deep into the psyche, to dip into the creative waters of the subconscious. Is the fact of structure an essential element in the creative lives of Christian women? Then what of the vast numbers of Christian women who are not in convents? Those married and raising children? What of single women? What of the contemporary challenge facing women today, of balancing work and home?

I began to think about the relationship of structure

to creativity in its many forms, and its relationship to women's history. If in the past creativity developed within well-defined boundaries, how is it happening today as boundaries are constantly shifting? Are there new structures of creativity?

As I thought about the question, it seemed to me that women's creativity has been enhanced by structures that:

- allow for spiritual exploration by providing time and space and study opportunities;
- evoke community, where life can be shared and consciousness enlarged;
- articulate a common purpose or common cause;
- provide opportunities for solitude where the soil of creativity can be cultivated, where seeds barely formed can take root and be protected and nourished until strong enough to become visible.

I approach the topic of women and creativity from the perspective of structure and I do so in three ways. First is a discussion of the nature of creativity, and especially the place of courage in a truly creative life. The second discussion consists of some reflections on structures that have fostered Christian women's creativity, namely religious life (convents), domestic life (the home), and the women's movement (beyond home and convent). The third part involves speculation on a new structure, one that is large enough and accommodating enough to house both women religious and lay women, what I am calling in this lecture a new home, a home of accumulated wisdom.

In her poem "The House of the Silver Spirit," Jessica Powers writes: "I think this house broke from some

4

wild travail," and she goes on to speak of the "strange new miracle that came to be." Wisdom entered the house of the silver spirit; it nourished the poet's hopes and dreams; yet its singing soul did not deny suffering. What she says of her house of the silver spirit might be said of this new wisdom home envisioned by the women of the church. Built on foundations of the past and the wild travails of their experience, strange new miracles are possible.

1. COURAGE: THE FOUNDATION OF CREATIVITY

The psychotherapist Rollo May defines creativity as both the process of making or bringing into being (and here he echoes Webster) and the way we express our being.[5] Creative persons, according to May, are those who in some way enlarge human consciousness. They may do so in a variety of settings: the scientific laboratory, artistic studios, the schools of religion, in familial relationships. What seems key to May in the creative process is the encounter that occurs. Artists encounter the landscape they propose to paint; scientists confront their experiment; a child meets the dimensions of a game; a musician faces a score. In other words, the encounter is with one's world in which a certain quality of engagement occurs, a degree of intensity, a form of contemplative awareness, and as a result, consciousness is affected. The world does not mean simply environment. According to May it is "the pattern of meaningful relations in which a person exists and in the design of which he or she participates."[6] Encounter, engagement or participation and intensity or absorption are central terms in this preliminary discussion of creativity.

7

The participation which an encounter implies means that the breakthrough (the right poetic image, the perfect Picasso blue, the new hypothesis, the religious conversion) happens in the breaking up of old patterns and forms. What breaks up? It might be that to which we cling most rigidly in our individual conscious thinking or it might be what a lot of people believe is essential to the survival of their intellectual and spiritual world.[7] To critic George Steiner an intense encounter with one's world is a form of "annunciation . . . like gravity breaking into the small house of our cautionary beings."[8] The effect of such an annunciation, says Steiner, is "that the house is no longer habitable in quite the same way as it was before."[9]

Because the house of our being, individually and collectively, is threatened by creative insight and application, both commitment and courage are needed to combat anxiety and guilt. Commitment is demonstrated by one's presence to the task or the cause, the presence of time and concentration, the discipline of preparation and work. The insight or new awareness or new idea will usually arise at a moment of transition between work and relaxation, in the space between trying. However, abandoning the details of work and waiting for unconscious breakthroughs in ourselves or in others will not develop creativity. Take writers. They attest to sitting at their desks (or their word processors) daily, for specified periods of time, whether or not the Muse is active. Writing is their work and they submit to the discipline that requires.

Or consider teachers. Creative teachers—in all kinds of settings, but say those in inner-city schools—

8

know the value of lesson plans, including background preparation, that permit them to stand before a class of defensive, under-educated adolescents whose basic intelligence is impressive but repressed, and spontaneously ask questions that are drawn from what the students know about life. Jessica Seigel is a good example of what I mean. For a number of years Seigel taught in the Lower East Side of New York City. She taught American literature to today's young immigrants by cajoling them to tell their stories, the narratives of their own short lives, so that they might see the connections with the stories others have written, from Anne Bradstreet to F. Scott Fitzgerald—and not only written, but published. The encounters, when they happened, were electric. But they did not happen arbitrarily. Hard work, namely Seigel's planning and the students' own painstaking writing efforts, created the space for the wondrous fireworks when they appeared.

In Jessica Seigel's classroom, as in so many settings for creative encounters, the breakthrough occurred in the rest moment, when the guard was down. That moment, however, was preceded by disciplined effort which might go on for a very long time.[10] Undergirding such commitment is courage.

Again, Rollo May offers a comprehensive definition of courage as the capacity to move ahead in spite of despair. Such forward movement is possible because the person possesses a centeredness, what in the Christian tradition we would call contemplative awareness—that knowledge which inspired the writer of Acts to state the most fundamental fact of human existence: "In God we live and move and have our being" (Acts 17:28).

9

The courageous moving ahead takes different forms. One is what might be called moral courage, the abhorrence of violence and the identification through one's empathetic sensors with the sufferings of one's fellow human beings. This form of courage coursed through the pre-Glasnost gulags, preserved for us in a number of memoirs, in fiction and in poetry. Artists inhabited the gulags in large numbers because, as Rollo May notes, their vision and their courage always pose a threat to the status quo. Every society harbors fear of its artists, poets and saints, precisely because they see what new worlds are possible.[11] The historic events of the winter of 1989–1990 in eastern and central Europe were in a very real sense carried forward onto the world stage by the authentic creativity of the artistic community there. The vision of Poland's Solidarity movement was largely formed in the images of C. Milosz, whose poems are engraved on the Solidarity monuments in Gdansk, as well as in the hearts of the Polish people. Writer Vaclav Havel's deep understanding of the moral weight of the uttered word coupled with his commitment to truth revealed him as leader, not only to the people of Czechoslovakia, but to the people of the world. Hungary's poet-president, Arpad Goncz, can lead his country because, among many factors, he communicates bone-true experience. These new leaders have been formed in suffering. Their courage is like music: the sound never dies.

Poet Irina Ratushinskaya's story illustrates the essence of the creative courage of a new generation of visionary leaders in eastern-central Europe. Arrested because her poems were judged to be a danger to the

10

state, this young Soviet (and Christian) woman, on the day before her 29th birthday, was sentenced to seven years hard labor. For three years she was held in Small Zone, a special unit for women prisoners of conscience. Her poetry continued because poetry is not something one does, an option among many others. It is a way of life. In the words of May Sarton, it is "a life discipline . . . maintained in order to perfect the instrument of experiencing—the poet himself [sic]—so that he may learn to keep himself perfectly open and transparent, so that he [sic] may meet everything that comes his way with an innocent eye."[12]

Irina Ratushinskaya distilled the experience of the Small Zone into poems, some of them first written with burnt matchsticks onto bars of soap and then memorized; others copied in tiny letters onto strips of paper which were hidden and then smuggled out of camp. Her poems embody the forward movement of creative courage.

Above my half of the world
The comets spread their tails.
In my half of the century
Half the world looks me in the eye.
In my hemisphere the wind's blowing,
There are feasts of plague without end.
But a searchlight shines in our faces,
And effaces the touch of death.
And our madness retreats from us,
And our sadness passes through us,
And we stand in the midst of our fates,
Setting our shoulders against the plague.

We shall hold it back with our selves,
We shall stride through the nightmare.
It will not get further than us—don't be afraid
On the other side of the globe![13]

Can you feel the bonds of moral goodness in those
final lines? The power that will stave off the flood of evil
westward? "We shall stride through the nightmare/It
will not get further than us—don't be afraid." Such
strong, brave, divinely hopeful hearts, the creative
among us, "forever unsatisfied with the mundane, the
apathetic, the conventional, they always push on to new
worlds. . . . They are the creators of the 'uncreated conscience of the race.' "[14] Furthermore, their forward
movement, through pain and despair, has form. The
creators arrange structures for communicating, for
carrying forward the seeds of new life. Rollo May goes
so far as to say that we have an active need for form, a
passion for form. "Insights emerge not chiefly because
they are intellectually true or even because they are
helpful, but because they have a certain form, the form
that is beautiful. . . ."[15]

It is the passion for form, beautiful form, that has
facilitated the creativity of women. Three structures in
particular seem to me to be unique for women's creativity, specifically for Christian women: the convent or
monastery, the home, and the women's movement, particularly the small group, "extra domicile."

2. WOMEN'S PLACES:
STRUCTURES OF CREATIVITY

Until the last half of the twentieth century, women who were serious about their artistic vocations typically did not marry and have children. One need only begin a list of major women poets of the northern hemisphere—Emily Dickinson, Gabriela Mistral, Elizabeth Bishop, Marianne Moore—to name a few, and it is quickly evident that a common thread is their unmarried state. They were women who lived on the margins of convention. The same could be said of novelists, those in the fine arts, and scientific pioneers. The care and education of children, and the management of a home were rightly perceived as full-time jobs. Florence Nightingale, for example, was convinced that her vocation to nursing, something she understood as a call from God, precluded marriage.[16] Those who did marry, like George Eliot, did not pour energy into the cultural expectations surrounding marital relationships.[17]

CONVENT

For Catholic women who did not wish to marry and have children, who sensed their own creative impulses required a different kind of space than that of kitchen and parlor, life on the fringe of society was not a viable option. There was, however, a choice that could (and often did) support their spiritual/intellectual quest, and one which conveyed a certain status: they could enter the convent.[18]

For a very long time canon law recognized only one form of religious life for women—that of cloistered contemplative nuns with solemn vows as an authentic state of perfection. Yet dozens of new communities of women active in works of mercy and bound by simple vows appeared after the French Revolution. Their religious practice, heavily influenced by the monastic model, became a mixture of strict monastic practices and a response to contemporary need manifested in works of social compassion. These varied works themselves were a visible sign of creativity, one that will be discussed presently. But for a very long time the cloister was the premier alternative life-style for Catholic women, and one which afforded opportunities for creative development and expression. In the twelfth century Hildegard of Bingen, with her multifaceted giftedness is perhaps the best known prototype of creator-in-the-convent.[19]

Sor Juana Ines de la Cruz

Less well-known than Hildegard, but exquisitely illustrative of the connection between creativity and convent is Sor Juana Ines de la Cruz, widely regarded by critics of Spanish literature as one of the great poets of seventeenth-century New Spain—Mexico. For centuries she has puzzled many who studied her life and her accomplishments.

Juana Ines lived at the royal court in Mexico City from ages sixteen to twenty, a favorite of the Vicereine. Her beauty, intellectual acumen, and literary gifts were greatly admired. By all accounts she lived fully the life of the court, participating in entertainments and diversions, including flirtations and amorous theatrical plays. At the height of her courtly pleasures, at age nineteen, she entered a cloistered Carmelite convent, but after a brief time there, she returned to the world, probably because the Carmelite way of life was too rigorous for her. But a year-and-a-half later she took her vows in an order much milder in discipline, the Hieronymite Order.

Mexican writer and Nobelist Octavio Paz, in his stunning study of this extraordinary woman, considers the possible reasons for this unexpected and hard-to-explain decision in her life.[20] First there is her background. She was illegitimate and so did not have the security of family and dowry (although she knew her mother's family, and was indebted to her grandfather for sparking her love of learning). But her irregular family situation and the consequent lack of dowry was an obstacle to a suitable marriage. Still, she was well-regarded at court, and who knows what might have been arranged? Paz lays the family situation aside. He sees a different reason.

While it seems quite reasonable to him that she might have fallen in love while she lived in the palace, and while it is indisputable that she lacked family position and a dowry, her choice of the convent does not seem "second best" to Paz. Juana herself gives what to Paz is a most plausible reason for her choice: she felt no inclination toward marriage.

Paz is careful to make a distinction between love and matrimony, which, in the seventeenth century, were quite separate. There are women, he reminds us, who choose to avoid the married state, which does not, however, rule out love. But marriage at that time, and in those circumstances, was not conducive to the pursuit of the intellectual, artistic, aesthetically creative life. While not denying the authenticity of Sor Juana's religious vocation, he situates it in a human context, namely, the need to find a haven for herself to develop her talents, a place respectable and secure. Her eagerness for knowledge was paramount. She writes in a document called *Response* the following passage:

> And so I entered the religious order, knowing that life entailed certain conditions (I refer to superficial, and not fundamental, circumstances) most repugnant to my nature; but given the total apathy I felt toward marriage, I deemed convent life the least unsuitable and the most honorable I could elect if I were to ensure my salvation. To that end first (as, finally, the most important) was the matter of all the trivial aspects of my nature . . . , such as wishing to live alone, and wishing to have no obligatory occupation to inhibit the freedom of my studies, nor the sounds of a community

16

to intrude upon the peaceful silence of
my books.[21]

Paz categorizes her reasons, then, as negative (her antip-
athy toward marriage and her need for a refuge from
the difficulties of a woman alone in the world), and posi-
tive (her attraction for learning). As a child she steeped
herself in her grandfather's library, devouring books, all
kinds of books, unknown to her family. That love of
knowledge deepened with the years. To be faithful to
the inner call to know and to write, she needed something that the convent could offer—solitude. It was not
a solitude of total isolation, but one that allowed for
intellectual communication. Sor Juana was engaged in a
far ranging and continuing correspondence with the
outside world for which, it must be admitted, she was
censured. Still, the right combination of solitude, communication and learning was available to her in the convent of St. Jeronimo.

The dynamics of solitude and a community of
shared interest are, I believe, essentials of the creative
life. Solitude, as poet May Sarton notes, "cracks open
the inner world."[22] Creative leaders, thinkers, artists—
these seem especially marked and strengthened by solitude. Catherine of Siena in her room voluntarily cut off
from the social intercourse of her home, John of the
Cross in the Tower, Florence Nightingale on her
sickbed, Malcolm X in solitary confinement, Van Gogh
in Arles, Nelson Mandela in a South African prison, and
of course, Jesus in the desert—for all these and so many
more, unseen solitude offered a spaciousness where the

17

secrets of the soul could be explored and given form. Sor Juana's convent was such a place. But there was a level of contrast present also.

In many ways St. Jeronimo resembled a small city. Each nun had a cell that was in reality a small apartment, complete with kitchen, bathroom and sitting room and often occupying two floors. Servants and slaves (who could be sold) were part of the tiny households within the larger organization of the convent. Even the habits —conventual dress—were more elegant than humble. Jewelry often was worn. Visitors (theologians, homilists, members of the court, in addition to family) were frequent, remaining in special "speak rooms" after Vespers. Visits sometimes inspired performance of some type—dancing, singing, recitation, theatrical scenes, usually performed by the girls studying with the nuns. It would seem that visitors were refreshed in the style of the true salon.

Religious structure was, of course, observed. There was a daily horarium of prayer which included mass, lauds, the daytime hours of prayer, vespers and compline. The prayer moments were, in fact, the substance of the nuns' common life. Meals were rarely taken in common, the nuns preferring their cells and the culinary skills of their particular servants. Apparently time was available for individual interests like sewing, painting and crafts. In Paz's view these and other avenues of continued learning and creative expression were essential for mental health in the convents. And while the convents of New Spain were not on a par with the monasteries, or particularly with the Jesuit houses of study, according to Paz, for someone with Sor Juana's intellect, energy and aesthetic sensibilities, her convent was uniquely suited to her development. Poetry and plays, secular and religious, flowed from her cell and were carried beyond the borders of Mexico. Most of her work was published in Spain, and was recognized then, as now, as something of value. One sees this first in her sonnets. Paz calls attention to the sonnet images which transcend time and cultures. One remarkably modern image is that of the writer who sees herself writing:

> Unhappy lyre whereon your music played,
> be still, its echoes call to you in pain,
> misshapen are the letters that here fall,
> black teardrops from my melancholy pen.[23]

Sor Juana matches May Sarton's delineation of the poet as one who lives a life of disciplined awareness so that everything may be met with an innocent eye, a state of being on the edge of mysticism.[24] Years of lauds and vespers help to expose one's being. But the prayer of the church, the seclusion of her cell and stimulating correspondence were not all that nourished Sor Juana's inner life and light. Like Sarton, centuries later, the poet Sor Juana developed through the friendship of women, within and without the convent.[25] Not only did these friendships fulfill psychic needs but probably ushered in Sor Juana's Muse as well.

More startling than her twentieth-century poetic images, her volume of work and her web of relationships, were Sor Juana's feminist writings, almost impossible to imagine in the seventeenth century in a society whose ethos was shaped by a combination of Arabic and Roman-Christian beliefs and customs regarding women.[26] In one poetic satire Sor Juana questions the dual standards applied to women and men regarding sexual behavior. Why do men insist on blaming women, she asks? Does not the sexual act almost inevitably result from masculine initiative? She was not the first person to raise these arguments, but she was the first woman of literature to do so with intelligence and grace. "There is nothing similar in literature by women in 17th century France, Italy, or England," says Paz.[27]

Her feminism reached beyond sexual behavior, however. She wrote admiringly of learned women, those of pagan times as well as Christian times. In defense of her own pursuit of learning, under scrutiny by the Holy Office, she addressed herself to the question of what the Pauline text about women keeping silent in the churches really meant, and she concluded that women may study, interpret and teach holy scripture, although not from the pulpit, but rather in their homes and in private places. And, in fact, she argues for something akin to universal education for women to include secular subjects as well as sacred ones.[28] Sor Juana's life and work invite further study and reflection.

Mother Austin Carroll

The creativity fostered by convent life is not only of the explicitly artistic or intellectual kind. The culture of vowed religious life, especially in the fresh newness of America, sparked other kinds of creative instincts. Mary Ewens's comprehensive essay "Women in the Convent," which appears in *American Catholic Women*, personalizes a number of remarkable nineteenth-century apostolic women religious. Among them are Cornelia Connolly, who separated from her husband so he could become a priest, and who then founded her own religious community of women; Katherine Drexel who used her personal fortune to support her community's mission to Afro-Americans and Native Americans; St. Frances Xavier Cabrini, an educational pioneer, and many, many more. I was especially struck by the story of Mother Austin Carroll, a Sister of Mercy, who illustrates in a different way from Sor Juana, the relationship between convent and creativity. Furthermore, her story is representative of the kinds of experiences that were common to many women of that period, according to Ewens.

Born in County Tipperary in 1835, she joined the Sisters of Mercy in Cork in 1853. She was, at age eighteen, certified to teach. As a novice she was exposed to various kinds of social needs and acquired the skills necessary to care for those needs, learning what Ewens describes as "the Mercy method," a process that today we would call empowerment: teaching people what they need to know to help themselves.

In 1856 Sister Austin Carroll arrived at the Providence, Rhode Island, mission of the Sisters of Mercy prepared to undertake a variety of teaching assignments, including teaching in parochial schools, industrial schools and Sunday schools. Over the years her service extended in other directions as well—to soup kitchens, a home for women, and a day-care center for children of working women. She also nursed Civil War veterans from both North and South. In 1869 she moved south, to a beginning mission in New Orleans. Again, the scope of Sr. Carroll's service and ministry grew. Her considerable energies and talents went to home visits to the sick, prison ministry, a home for women, an employment bureau, a food pantry, and a clothing center for the poor.[29] To read through Mother Carroll's accomplishments is to recognize a woman who quickly sized up the needs of a particular place or group of people and who responded to the situation with decisiveness and imagination. She truly encountered her environment, bringing creative courage to bear on the various segments of human need to which she was drawn.

Nowhere was Mother Carroll's creativity more evident than in the number of schools that were opened in the south by the time of her death in 1909. The schools were an American experiment of sorts, democratic in values while stressing excellence in education. Some of the schools were "pay or select schools" and the income derived from tuition in these schools allowed the Sisters of Mercy to carry on their work with the poor, a support method utilized by many religious communities.

Like others with creative vision, new possibilities kept appearing on Mother Carroll's personal horizon. One possibility, one "dream," was to establish an institution of higher education for women, and indeed in 1887 she purchased land and put up a building for that purpose. But according to Ewens, the New Orleans clergy were "aghast at the idea of the Church promoting higher education for women" and they successfully blocked the project.[30]

Other projects must have appeared less threatening to the status quo: they survived and thrived. One of the most innovative Carroll projects was her House of Mercy where immigrant women and widows, among others, were taught related skills according to the needs of the job market. Jobs were then found through the employment bureau. One can see here a blueprint for the Great Society's Job Corps, established almost a century later.

In addition to her own version of creative community action, Austin Carroll wrote and translated books and wrote for newspapers and magazines. At the World's Exposition held in New Orleans in 1884–85, twenty-two of the forty-five works on display in the women's literary department were hers. In one, a translation of the life of St. Margaret Mary Alacoque, she wrote in the introduction about the qualities historically found in convents: "Not only do we find the chronicle of religious congregations . . . replete with everything gentle and holy, we find too among these . . . exotics of the Church—when occasion requires—a patient endurance, an invincible energy, an unconquerable activity. . . ."[31] A precise if paraphrased rendering of Rollo May's description of creative courage.

In the twentieth century the creative energies of vowed religious life began to focus in a serious and systematic way on higher education for women. Many sisters had the opportunity to study in secular universities and to pursue specialized study in music and the arts, both in America and in Europe. With the Second Vatican Council's invitation for religious congregations to discover anew their original charisms, American sisters seriously applied both gospel principles and the American pioneering spirit to their own renewal. The result has been an application of their expertise and their creativity to the problems of our time: racism, sexism, poverty and other problems affecting contemporary women. If there is one common theme coursing through the decades of renewal in religious life it would seem to be that of putting into practice the preferential option for the poor articulated with such passion at the gathering of Latin American bishops at Pueblo and at Medellin.

Clearly convent life today is markedly different from that of Sor Juana's time or even Mother Carroll's. Still, the vowed religious way of life with its intentional prayer, dedication to gospel values, mutual support, openness to new pathways of service remains a sturdy structure for the creativity of Christian women. Solitude, which fostered creativity in earlier convent times, is still a part of vowed life. It is not unusual for women religious, particularly those engaged in scholarly work, to live alone. Community, too, has new shapes and forms. Small communities of women, often engaged in different missions and ministries, are more the norm than not. Members may even be from different parent communities and congregations. In these new settings alternative ways of life for Christian women are being designed.[32] These experiments in community life and

24

work may indeed reach beyond the convent, to influence other dimensions of Christian organization.

At Home: Domestic Creativity

If the convent offered women who wanted an intellectual or artistic life a place to live out that impulse in a systematic and sustained way within the Christian ethos, then the vast majority of Christian women who could not or would not function in convent settings had to have some other avenues for creativity. The western world and the Christian world, so closely intertwined, shared a perspective of how Christian womanhood was to be lived out, namely, in seclusion, under the protection of males. Within post-Reformation Catholic Christianity convents not only complied with that view, but they strengthened it by designating vowed religious life a way of life that led to perfection (the designation finally being determined by the hierarchy). Marriage and family life, homemaking, was the other pole around which most women joined their lives: circumscribed, enclosed to some extent, with the norms for conduct and behavior determined in much the same way as they were for convents. One other option remained—that of single life, usually lived in the family home. It was an option not generally valued by society. Yet creative work was possible with this choice, and we can see the fruitfulness of that way of life in Emily Dickinson's rare verses, Florence Nightingale's nursing reforms, Maria Montessori's revolutionizing of early childhood education, and Jane Addams' building of women's solidarity across class lines. And there is Dorothy Day who, after the birth of her daughter, did not marry but put her intellectual and spiritual gifts, and her uncommon courage, at the service of the Catholic Worker movement which she helped found. Single women all.

It may be argued that there have been married women who devoted themselves to intellectual and artistic callings. Usually, however, these women were married to supportive and nurturing men, as in the case of Virginia and Leonard Woolf in this century. Or they shared a common calling with their husbands, like Raissa and Jacques Maritain. And for the most part such marriages were childless.

The Catholic Home

But the Catholic ideal of marriage included children, flesh and blood progeny, not literary legacies. Furthermore, in the United States, at least, this ideal was influenced by Victorian mores. And Victorian women were not encouraged to develop commitments outside of their domestic responsibilities.

Colleen McDannell situates the merging of two ideologies of domesticity, Catholic and Protestant Victorian, in the person of the Irish maid, employed in American Victorian homes. "Irish women, many of whom had no contact with Victorian domestic ideology before leaving Ireland, learned from their Protestant mistresses how a 'good' woman acted and what a 'good' family looked like."[33] The "good" family lived in clean, well-ordered and heavily populated households.

From the mid-nineteenth century to the second quarter of the twentieth a common, cohesive domestic ideology held sway, and in Catholic homes the ideology was reinforced by European biases, mostly French, about what constituted piety and good manners. The resulting Catholic-Victorian ideology was communicated by what McDannell calls the Catholic elite. The written word and the preached word, especially in Irish churches, held up the image of the home as a sacred school for the production of good Catholics, and the role of lay women was to strengthen family bonds by every means available, including entertainment such as music, games and group activities. The idealized image of domesticity wrongly assumed that women did not work outside the home, and so, according to the literature and the preaching, the work ethic was to flourish within the home. "The useful art of making shirts and mending stockings and managing household affairs" was equated with a happy home.[34] The truth is that large numbers of women *did* work elsewhere and returned home at day's end to try to live up to the prevalent image. The result was often exhaustion.

According to McDannell Irish women traditionally enjoyed a certain authority in the home. This might be traced to late marriages and to the tendency to same-sex bonding: the men socialized with men, the women with women. French Catholicism was different. It introduced household-based patriarchy into the Catholic domestic ideology as it was taking shape in the United States. The influence came largely through books, religious articles and religious practices. In this model male authority was unquestioned, and was cast in the context of religious ordering, a reflection of God's relationship with the people and with the church. Given all of this, whether French or Irish, the Catholic presentation of marriage and family life held up the woman as a kind of savior whose daily household duties provided her with a religious pathway at once secure and interesting. The Blessed Virgin Mary and women saints were the Catholic woman's "support group," accompanying her on the way to religious and spiritual formation at home. The domestic church, while not named as such, was in fact the ideal Catholic home, and unlike the European idealization, the American version did not insist on the father as the priest of the "domestic church." That role could be fulfilled by both parents or even by the mother alone.[35]

The domestic space often reflected the devotional life of the family with images of the Sacred Heart in the kitchen, a crucifix in each bedroom, a May altar to honor Mary complete with statue or other image and fresh flowers, and in some cases a photograph of the pope displayed in one of the home's public rooms. I remember the Sunday dinners of my childhood, midday after the last mass, seated at our dining room table opposite a framed photo of Pius XII, which hung on the wall. By the time I was thirteen my own bedroom housed a collection of saints' statues—my favorites— which I lined up at night before my night prayers.[36]

But the maintenance of household shrines and the culture of piety was especially pronounced in Mexican families where the woman—wife and mother—created the family's spiritual, familial and cultural place of remembering. Religious and family objects appeared together at household altars, and indeed, the saints honored in a particular family were considered part of the family.[37]

Italian religious domesticity was similar to the Mexican. For both groups the home, not the parish, was the center of religious life. The Poles were different. Polish immigrants to America associated themselves quickly and closely with the parish, most of which were national parishes with Polish language and customs. And even though household shrines and home piety were part of the culture, the parish was the center of religious and social life, and priests were held in high regard. American Catholicism's strong identification with the parish may be traced in part to this particular ethnic influence.

By the 1950s the literature of Catholic domesticity was still emphasizing the authority of the father in the home, an authority that was moral, religious and practical, while the role of the mother was to create a well-organized and religious home. This domestic ideology which seems today to be rigidly narrow in terms of gender role in the family helped, in fact, to promote a lay-oriented American Catholicism. McDannell holds that the idealization of Catholic domesticity weakened the preference for the celibate life as the premier way of perfection as it had been expressed in traditional Catholicism.[38] Women were empowered to "save" their families because "they fully embraced an otherworldly outlook. They were selfless, obedient, charitable, modest, and cloistered in their homes."[39] This domestic ethos did not engender a church or a nation of passive women, however. McDannell sees the idealization of Catholic woman in America, placing her in fact as spiritual and religious leader of the home, as creating a wedge in the patriarchal framework of the home, and ultimately doing the same in the wider church.

The domestic sphere, then, allowed Catholic laywomen to develop their potential as religious leaders. The fruitfulness of that particular form of creativity is evident in today's organizational church life. The vast range of church mission, from catechetics to schooling, from health care to social work is, in fact, in the hands of laywomen.[40]

Quakers

If Catholic laywomen came to a sense of equal participation through their theology of home, Quaker women did so through their fundamental belief in the spiritual equality of men and women, a concept embedded in the foundations of the Society of Friends. The practical consequences of this articulated belief in equality was the intentional training of women for leadership. In meetings of Friends, wives and mothers preached, took minutes, wrote epistles and conducted the meetings. The meeting house experience, in effect, prepared women for leadership in civil communities.

Equality was also practiced in Quaker homes. Men and women shared domestic tasks and responsibilities; there was equal education and the opportunities for careers for women. Operative equality in the home served to free women—and men—for creative undertakings on behalf of social justice. Many streams of social reform have benefitted from the Quaker experience, including the women's movement.[41]

The Frontier

The at-home creativity of women found an explicitly artful expression on the frontier. Not only did frontier women and settlers embody courage and ingenuity in the creation of homes under difficult circumstances, they perfected a new art, that of quilt making.

Patricia Cooper and Norma Bradley Allen have given a moving account of the relationship of quilting to the lives of the quilters they interviewed for an oral history of the art and the artists.[42] Their study of the quilters underscored the fact that, in addition to being records of family and community history, and a repository of American design and textiles, quilts were also art coming directly out of the home, out of family interactions. "The home was studio, art school, and gallery," they write.[43]

Cooper and Allen note how the art was controlled and handed down by women. This handing down was itself an educative process involving tradition, discipline, planning, and moral reinforcement. Since materials on the frontier were often scarce, inventiveness was called for. As soon as a girl was old enough she received her "piece bag" where she kept little scraps of fabric, pieces of wool, or whatever could be used in the work of art yet to be born. Girls kept their piece bags into old age.

Quilting was not only an artistic statement, but also a philosophic expression as well. We see that in the re-

31

flections of one elderly quilter interviewed for the oral history. "You can't always change things. Sometimes you don't have no control over the way things go. Hail ruins crops, or fire burns you out. And then you're given just so much to work with in a life and you have to do the best you can with what you got. That's what piecing is. The materials is passed on to you or is all you can afford to buy . . . that's just what's given to you. Your fate. But the way you put them together is your business. You can put them in any order you like."[44]

Another woman, Mrs. Wilman, remembered stories her mother told her about traveling from Springfield, Missouri, to the plains of West Texas as a bride. She set out in a covered wagon with one bedstead and a lamp and all the quilts she had made for her hope chest. Tools, seed and utensils for the house filled several trunks. During the long journey the new bride worked out of her "piece bag" making a Star of Bethlehem quilt which still remains in the family. Her first home was a dugout house, underground. There, in the dugout, Mrs. Wilman said, her mother made the best quilts "because that was when she needed something pretty."[45] Through dust storms, through loneliness when her husband was away, through worry about her endangered gardens, through her desire to raise her children in a house above ground, the woman in the dugout quilted. It was as if this pioneer woman built a base with her quilts and used them as a plan for her next project, an above-ground house. The authors use the image of roots to describe her creative courage and fortitude. "At each step she sank her roots deeper into the earth. At each level she changed, built her surroundings. She structured her surroundings. . . . Then the community came next. Roots reaching out from one ranch to the next, from one house to the next . . . a whole network, grid of support."[46] The story of Mrs. Wilman's mother is not unlike the stories of countless pioneer women, kept company by their silent friends, the piece bags, through lonely and difficult periods.

Churches often figured in the quilting history of families and communities. People would gather at churches for communal quilting, and often the motivation for a quilt came from something in the congregational life of a particular place of worship. "You know this quilt we did for our Bible teacher? It was just out of love and appreciation for her. She taught us the Bible once a week, we didn't pay or nothing. She taught because she was so full of it and she just couldn't get enough of talking about it. Anybody that wanted to come could come. She just loved to teach the Bible so well."[47]

Quilts launched marriages, announced babies and put homes back together after fire or trouble. For pioneer women quilts were the bearers of their lives, even those that were slightly unconventional. "Lord knows, honey, I never quilted when I was a child. Not me. I was the one ran outside and stayed gone most of the day until I was old enough to work. Then I took up working in the fields alongside the men. I was always the big woman and I couldn't be cooped up in no house. Why I never picked up a needle except to mend until I was sixty-five and took to quilting. Now I can't stop. Everything I ever learned about building and plowing goes into these quilts. Except colors, them colors is all mine.

Now I like to try to put them colors down in a way no one every saw before."[48]

Quilting has survived industrialization, the Great Depression, and any number of wars great and small. In cabins and farmhouses, in Victorian parlors of towns and villages on the Eastern seaboard, in mid-western churches, in the great mountain ranges women have been working alone and together, in solitude and in community, "sewing into their quilts the history of their country and the quality of their lives."[49] Through quilting women could express support of the great moral, political and religious movements of different eras. That tradition continues to this day.

According to Sandi Fox the majority of American creations continue to be worked by women in domestic circumstances. "It is in the quilts made to celebrate those traditional moments associated with our rites of passage that the emotional parallels between nineteenth and twentieth-century quiltmakers and their work seems most unchanged. Quilts still mark the birth of a child, a marriage, or a death."[50] Among the most touching quilts are those known as mourning quilts, testaments of loss and grief. Some outstanding examples can be viewed at the Smithsonian Museum of American History in Washington, D.C.

The AIDS Memorial Quilt is a contemporary variation on the mourning quilt. These unjoined pieces worked by people all over the United States in memory of those who have died from this terrible disease, were brought to Washington D.C. and placed side-by-side on the mall, an icon of meditation and sorrow. Hundreds of thousands of men, women and children viewed the

34

quilt, which remains a powerful symbol of domestic creativity, a bridge from home to the larger world of human need and suffering. Quilts still tell the history of a time, a people, an event. Quilts still tell, in their designs, the stories of women.

The Women's Movement

The AIDS Memorial Quilt is a natural heir of women's domestic artistry which traditionally reflected the history of social change in our country. Over the years women have gathered in parlors, not only to quilt and to share tea and news, but also to discuss the pressing social issues of their times. The parlor was where women confronted the injustice of being denied the vote. The parlor was where their higher education needs were analyzed. The parlor was where the welfare of children was promoted. From the abolition of slavery to the establishment of just labor laws, women meeting in homes, (the sites of the early women's clubs) wove a strategy of intelligent and compassionate action. The history of twentieth-century America is very much the history of women creatively pressing for justice in society, and not only for themselves, but for children, and those most oppressed by sinful structures.

Women brought the memory and experience of the home into civic arenas. The creative movement for social change was from the parlor to the arena of political action.[51] One of the great alliances of this century was that of rich women of conscience and the tough women of the tenements, many of them immigrants, who together created a class-defying sisterhood that worked for peace, good government and social progress. This alliance of women was in truth the heart of the national reform movements of the twentieth century.

Jane Addams

Nowhere was the experience of home more imaginatively adapted to wider social needs than in Chicago, at Hull House, an experiment in women's social reform, under the leadership of Jane Addams. Hull House, situated in the heart of the most multiethnic, multicultural section of Chicago at that time (1889), drew strong-minded, energetic women who broke from their early training to be demure and submissive, to help organize the lower-class women who had been repressed, starved or beaten into submission. Jane Addams, a beneficiary of higher education, needed a purpose, a mission in life, and she believed that other young women (and men) from her class felt as she did. The educated idealists, like Jane Addams, were motivated to associate with the Settlement Movement (as the Addams reform/experiment came to be known) because of three trends. These were "the desire to add the social function to political democracy; to assist in the general progress of the race; and as an expression of Christianity through humanitarian activity."[52]

Hull House was first of all a center, a meeting place for the poor to connect with the resources that could improve their lives. And the resources were many: an art gallery/museum, a music school and theater, a public kitchen (the nineteenth-century version of a soup kitchen), and a Jane Club, which was a first link in a chain of organized women's labor. The Jane Club was first established for factory girls who themselves had the idea that a boarding club was needed for times of hardship, like strikes. The idea flowered and apartments near Hull House were rented. In May of 1891—one hundred years ago—fifteen young women moved in to live together on a cooperative basis. The idea grew, like so many of the Hull House projects.

Jane Addams's vision was ever expanding, moving her toward new engagements of courage and commitment. While in some sense, Hull House was always her home, her concern for peace linked her with women throughout the world, specifically through the Women's International League for Peace and Freedom, born out of the turmoil of the First World War. Her initiatives on behalf of peace were recognized in 1931 when she was awarded the Nobel Peace Prize (shared with Nicholas Murray Butler), the first woman to be so honored. Those who knew Jane Addams were not surprised that she donated her $16,000 prize money to the Women's International League for upkeep of its Geneva office.

Among the countless assessments of her life and accomplishments I find the one expressed in the *Christian Century* of June 5, 1935, most interesting. "She had no interest in descending to the poverty level. Her interest was in lifting the level of all about her to new heights. For that reason Hull House under her hand was always a place in which beauty was served, and the emphasis was on the maximum of enjoyment to be extracted from the widest possible spread of human interests and activities."[53] Jane Addams gave herself to the creation of the world family, a boundless family, in which regard for excellence was to be handed on from generation to generation. The light she and others enflamed has never been extinguished. In different and varied forms it has been passed on.

We have nothing which has not first been given us. The contemporary women's movement demonstrates that truth. The conscience, the spirit, the imagination, hard work, discipline, commitment and courage of women like Sor Juana, Mother Carroll, Jane Addams, the women of the frontier and those of the early women's clubs—all cultivated the ground of today's women's movement.

THE WOMEN'S MOVEMENT

How do terms like the "women's movement" or "feminism" fit into a Catholic ethos? In a book that brings the women's movement and Catholic social teaching into a civilized dialogue, Maria Riley, O.P., argues that feminism is really about the transformation of society into a more just order, and as such is central to the church's social mission.[54] She says this despite the fact that historically churches have been reluctant to promote major acquisitions of new rights for women. Cardinal Gibbons, for example, one of the acknowledged architects of Catholic social teaching publicly opposed women's suffrage, fearful that femininity would be lost if women were to enter the political arena, even if the arena were as small as a voting booth.[55] Could the cardinal ever imagine women as U.S. Senators, or state governors, or English prime ministers, one wonders?

When the Constitution was amended so that women could vote, the women's movement believed that equality was now a reality. Some in the movement realized, however, that suffrage was only a partial victory. They pointed out that women were still subordinated to men in most areas of daily and public life: in the professions, before the law and in various societal institutions, including the churches. Another amendment was needed, they said, one that would ensure equal rights beyond the voting booth.[56] The ERA, as the constitutional amendment was known, was approved by the House of Representatives and the Senate in 1972, forty years after it was introduced into Congress. As the amendment moved through the states in the ratification process, the women's movement was energized around a concrete goal. It served a similar function for those opposing the amendment. Catholics were among the supporters and the opponents, although traditional Catholic beliefs about family life, and women's role within that structure, seemed to favor the opposition. The ERA failed to win the necessary number of state ratifications, and while several individual bishops stated their support for the effort, as a body they did not do so, believing that support for the ERA could be interpreted as support for abortion. At this time the amendment seems to lack enthusiastic support in the Congress and in the country.

While the ERA was running its course, other facets of a growing feminism were influencing a wide spectrum of women in personal as well as political ways.

Prompted by the pioneers of the contemporary feminist movement in the sixties, women at that time began to meet in small groups, and there told their stories, engaging in what has come to be known as feminist analysis. That form of analysis locates the links in one's experience with patterns of oppression in one's life and with social structures which are in themselves discriminatory, not only of women but of all kinds of different others.

The experience of women in groups (as distinct from one-to-one relationships) has been a key factor in the women's movement.[57] A new phrase was crafted to describe the changes that occurred in groups—consciousness raising. Simply stated, consciousness raising meant that women—and men—began to see and to understand social relations and social institutions in a new way, and to speak about this new understanding with a depth of realization previously unknown.

At about the same time that the secular women's movement invited women (mainly) to venture from their privatized worlds into the larger world of group sharing, the Cursillo Movement, a Catholic awakening experience, that emphasizes the power of small Christian communities to affect positively the larger environment was growing in the United States. After the initial retreat which introduces the Cursillo method, cursillistos and cursillistas (men and women are segregated during the cursillo) are encouraged to continue to meet in small groups to keep the initial awakening alive and to deepen it. The existential encounter with Christ (in prayer, in scripture and in other people, especially in the poor) was and is primary in the small Cursillo group.

But in actuality, many women learned that in the search for Christ they discovered themselves as well, more honestly and more bravely than ever before. This two-part discovery is, in fact, a feature of Christian spirituality.[58]

Is "the group" to be equated with the structure of creativity in the women's movement? To a large extent, but not totally. The nature of the group is to provide boundaries, that is *a form* wherein listening, speaking, and shaping a narrative take on a life. Like the walls of a well, the group has enabled women to move to the level of life-giving water, to a level of new consciousness which Rollo May equates with essential creativity. The creative moment in every situation is precisely a break-through from the unconscious. May points out that what we cling to most rigidly in our conscious thinking is what breaks or shifts when consciousness expands, as the surface of the earth cracks when it quakes. And then, nothing is ever quite the same, as we see so clearly in the lives of mystics and inventors, artists and proph-ets. And we see it, too, close at hand, in the lives of mothers and nuns, students and workers, and wives. Within the framework of the church, the groups are of a rich variety, from study groups to mission groups to Cursillo groups, and so on. Women's lives are changed in these groups, and the world they touch is changed as well. Who are they?

One woman, dying of cancer, was bolstered by her women's group to continue with her painting and pho-tography to the end of her days. She left for all a legacy of beauty. Another woman, long a member of a Cursillo group, looked to the corporate wisdom of the group to help her decide if, in her mid-fifties, she could resume nursing in an inner-city religious health clinic. She did so and among her responsibilities is women's health education. Another finds strength in her group to respond with compassion and hope to the news that her son has AIDS, and now she is motivated to coordinate volunteers for the area's ecumenical AIDS ministry. Another leaves her group to study theology; she'll return someday. The stories go on and on. Some of them come from the consultation on the pastoral response to women's concerns. More than seven years ago local churches were asked by the National Conference of Catholic Bishops to hold listening sessions where women could voice their concerns. In this way the bishops believed the proposed pastoral letter would be rooted in the experience of women.

That process elicited accounts of courage and hope as well as tales of hurt and humiliation. The words of the women themselves form the heart of the first draft of the pastoral.[59] These voices of women which served as both commentary and illustration regarding the treatment of women in society and in the church, gave a unique tone to this church document.

The bishops' early invitation to honest dialogue allowed women, ordinary women from homes and offices and classrooms and parishes—not theologians—to relate their own experiences in matters of marriage and family, including issues of family planning and spousal equality; in matters of church ministry, both as volunteers and professional; in matters of social policy as it affects women. The process of *structured listening* enabled women of the church, laity and religious, to probe together the nature of their spirituality as women. Such probing in and of itself is an act of creativity. It becomes the encounter to which Rollo May refers, the encounter of the intensively conscious human being with her world.[60]

As a structure for creativity the women's movement shares some common ground with the convent and with the home. It shares in the bondedness that women experienced in convents and certainly in frontier homes. It shares the quality of self-direction. In both convent and home certain executive functions were needed and were developed in women, and these are evident in the movement. It shares the virtue of courage found in the counter-cultural ethos of the convent and in the frontier homes. Furthermore, the movement, like the convent and the home, has been fruitful, producing a large and growing body of scholarly research and works of art, ranging from feminist theology to painting, from linguistics to literature. In that way the movement has reached beyond the group to women everywhere. There seems a readiness for a new kind of home.

3. CREATING A NEW HOME: RELIGIOUS AND LAY WOMEN IN ALLIANCE

One of the most compelling images associated with the Second Vatican Council is that of Pope John XXIII metaphorically opening the windows of the church. One can imagine him calling for light and for air. Yet the dominant image in the generation since the council has not been that of the window, but rather of the pilgrimage. We have understood ourselves, as Christians, to be a people on the move, exploring, experimenting, and sometimes conquering. The pilgrimage or journey motif is rightly a part of our Christian history and our women's history. The women religious who ventured into uncharted mission lands, the women who settled the newest frontier, the women who marched in the streets for the right to vote, the women who came to the consultations for the women's pastoral determined to speak the truth and to test their own unique voices in deliberations and in prayer—for all of these the language of pilgrimage is pointedly apt.

But as Sharon Parks has suggested, the time has come for a companion image, and the one she suggests is that of home.[61] I believe that "home" is especially appropriate for the women of the church, women who carry with them the history of nuns, enclosed but still engaged in the life of the mind and the spirit; and the history of apostolic sisters, many of whom established homes for those adrift; and the history of domesticity and family where women often learned as much about politics as they did needlepoint, and then acted on what they learned.

It is not difficult to envision women religious and laywomen in a new alliance or partnership building a new house together, a home for the twenty-first century. There are already many indicators that such an alliance is possible.[62]

In the post-Vatican II years, as sisters moved from classroom teaching to leadership in non-school religious education, they became the daily pastoral presence in parishes. The DRE not only organized the children's programs and supported the volunteer catechists, she offered counsel and encouragement to the mothers, many of whom were at home during the day. Frequently, laywomen were drawn into ministry by the DRE who knew what women could accomplish.

The daughters of the catechists and liturgical planners of the 60s are now studying in schools of theology, from Berkeley to Boston. They are a new generation of women who came to the theologate because of intellectual interest, or experience in mission of some kind (the Jesuit volunteers, for example), or because of a retreat, or maybe the influence of a friend—or a memory of their mothers and aunts and neighbors immersed in CCD and growing in Christian faith and commitment through that experience. Or their mothers and aunts, now free of home responsibility, may have preceded them to the theologate. Whenever I meet with women who are studying theology I am struck by the age range: grandmothers and women in their 20s share a common passion for learning about God. These women speak of being called by God to serve the church and the world, and they are trying to be faithful to the call, often at great personal sacrifice, with little if any institutional support. They wonder, more in puzzlement than anger, that the church seems not to notice them, and by that they mean officialdom, the diocesan center, or perhaps the conference of bishops. When their studies are completed they are as likely to work in a Catholic Worker house or a safe house for battered women as they are in a parish. They are not concerned about recognition or status, but about connectedness. Sisters, who are frequently in programs with them, are a source of understanding. They *are* institutionally connected, by virtue of their canonical status, and they will often assume the role of welcomer.

Bonds between sisters and laywomen have been strengthened also through the ministry of spiritual direction. Religious have shared what they know about the rich spiritual heritage preserved in Catholic Christianity, and they have encouraged women to follow the interior way.

The vast arena of social concerns, from political research and lobbying to direct service to the poor, has brought religious and laity into communities of shared concern and ongoing action.

For a generation now, laywomen and women religious have invested the word "sisterhood" with new

46

meaning. This relatively new and increasingly vibrant relationship is the raw material for the home I propose. In this home women will contribute what they have learned and preserved from the other places of memory and history: the inventiveness of the pioneer home, the spiritual knowledge of the convent, the class transcendence of the settlement houses, the analytic skills of the contemporary women's movement, and so much more. Of course there would not be a single "home"—I am talking about shared experience as much as I am about place—but there might be centers, gathering places for women, and men, where a contemporary spirituality could be cultivated. Prayer and silence would be needed, and the kind of dialogue that Jesuit sociologist John Coleman calls "a new kind of talking." By that he means bringing the content of one's work and relationships, the content of the social structures in which we live into the light of the scriptures, and to name what, in the midst of all the complexity and disappointments and failures, gives us hope. You will see a naming of God in such exercises.

Imagine for a moment the placement of a window in this home, perhaps a window like good Pope John had in mind. The window allows light to fill the interior of the home, and it will be important to look within, to note carefully the condition of the interior. We must be mindful of beauty, so that the space within attracts and includes. And we must be mindful of peace.

The window also opens out onto the world. Through the window we see the signs of our time on earth, the signs we have been asked to read and to interpret. (Gaudium et Spes #62) Three signs of need are immediately visible to me. They call for the creativity of women developed over these many centuries. I want to briefly comment on them. (Each deserves many lectures and books!)

CARE FOR THE EARTH

In the fall of 1990 fifty women met at the United Nations Church Center to establish a worldwide network for bringing their agenda into the environmental debate. In particular they asked to be represented at the United Nations Conference on Environment and Development in Brazil in 1992. The women came from diverse cultures in Latin America, Africa, Asia, Europe and North America, and while their advocacy styles differed, they were in agreement concerning their goals. Their plan of action included full participation by women in environment policy at all levels, increased education and information on the environment and development of a code of earth ethics, freedom of choice in family planning and redefinition of development.[63]

I submit that Christian women, in particular an alliance of Catholic religious and laity, have much to bring to the worldwide debate. Respect for the earth is an important strain of the contemplative tradition. Celtic spirituality, the Benedictine principle of working the earth, Franciscan simplicity, the women mystics of the Middle Ages, the cosmic vision of Teilhard de Chardin —we have resources to offer. Closer at hand the work of Passionist father Thomas Berry cries out to Christian conscience—to all conscience—to recognize our rela-

48

tionship to the earth. Jane Blewett, a disciple of Berry's, has begun a center for research and education in the Washington D.C. area to help those of us who look out the window to respond to the cry of the earth: to the polluted air, the disintegrating ozone shield, the ground water pollution, the disappearing songbirds. What would life be like without the birds of the air?

I can go starved the whole day long,
draining a stone, eating a husk,
and never hunger till a song
breaks from a robin's throat at dusk.

I am reminded only then
how far from day and human speech,
how far from the loud world of men
lies the bright dream I strain to reach.

Oh, that a song of mine could burn
the air with beauty so intense,
sung with a robin's unconcern
for any mortal audience!

Perhaps I shall learn presently
his secret when the shadows stir,
and I shall make one song and be
aware of but one Listener.[64]

Women know the value of small actions as well as coordinated, corporate efforts. St. Thérèse's "little way" is poignantly applicable to our mission to the earth; and the Earthworks Group points to all the ways each of us can make a difference, can show compassion for our larger home.[65]

For centuries women of the convent have raised their voices in psalms that glorify God. They know that wind and rain and earth and sky give glory to God. Their voices are needed today; we need to join with them.

TRUE PARTNERSHIP BETWEEN MEN AND WOMEN

When writer Francine du Plessix Grey went to the Soviet Union several years ago to conduct in-depth interviews with women there, she was surprised at what she found.[66] In a society that claimed total equality between women and men, Grey learned that an enormous abyss existed between the sexes. As she asked women about their families and their work, about their spiritual values and about what was precious to them, she found men were not in the women's priorities. Significant relationships tended to be those of mother and daughter, teacher and student, friends. Much of this alienation, she observes, is traceable to a lack of shared responsibility on the part of men in domestic life, with the resulting burden of outside work and home responsibility exhausting the women. After one or two children are born, the women are content to get on with their lives—alone.

The U.S. Catholic bishops' women's pastoral (both drafts) urges that partnership be developed in marriages and in family life.[67] And while the Soviet solution (or lack of solution) is not visible through the metaphorical window, there are issues of communication and patterns of working and living that need attention. As more and more mothers work outside the home (and the numbers are increasing) how to share home and child care is crucial. Heightened understanding of how the socialization of girls and boys affects our capacities to communicate as men and women is also needed.

Deborah Tannen, a professor of linguistics at Georgetown University, has unexpectedly been on the N.Y. Times best-seller list with a book about the differences in gender communication, called *You Just Don't Understand*.[68] Dr. Tannen contends different patterns of socialization among girls and boys lead to different patterns of communication, at all levels. She notes that boys' play is organized in a hierarchical way: there is a leader of the team who gives the signals and the orders and solves the problems. Girls, on the other hand, tend to decide in a group. They have "best friends" in whom they confide, and with whom they can talk for hours.

In adulthood, Dr. Tannen says, these patterns persist. The "leader" knows what to do, and how to do it, and any threat to that sense of competence creates a lot of problems. Another leadership design—say that favored in the women's movement, one of peer leadership—is not often found in the social institutions of society, although it is present in religious communities of women, and increasingly in diocesan commissions on women.

The difference in socialization creates communication impasses. An example will illustrate. A woman says to her husband (or to the priest on her ministerial team), "I have a problem." She starts to talk about it,

51

and very quickly the man says, "Well, this is what you should do." And then he gives her a solution, which is not what she wanted. She wanted to talk about it, and wanted him to listen as much as to talk—all of which you will recognize as a distinctively pastoral activity. The point is they are missing each other.

As Christians our vocation is one of reconciliation, and ongoing reconciliation between women and men, in all spheres of life, seems to me to be part of that vocation. Furthermore, when one begins an examination of the spiritual reforms within the church, the partnership of men and women in these reforms is quickly evident. Francis and Clare. Catherine of Siena and Raymond of Capua. John of the Cross and Teresa of Avila. Jane Frances de Chantal and Francis de Sales. In our own time, Father Thomas Judge and Margaret Healy, founders of the Missionary Cenacle Apostolate; and Peter Maurin and Dorothy Day. The list is extensive.

Can we not in our new home practice the skills and the virtues that can fashion an authentic partnership between men and women? Our ancient virtues of truthfulness and humility (in its true sense, not in aberrant ways), of fortitude and perseverance are needed. Deep listening is needed, as the poet Milosz listened one day in a Berkeley cafeteria:

> My parents, my husband, my brother, my sister
> I am listening in a cafeteria at breakfast
> The women's voices rustle, fulfill themselves
> In a ritual no doubt necessary.
> I glance sidelong at their moving lips
> And I delight in being here on earth

For one more moment, with them, here on
  earth
To celebrate our tiny, tiny, my-ness.[69]

CHILDREN'S ADVOCACY AND CARE

Through the window one sees the children of the
earth, our children; they are in great peril. In some
ultimate sense we create a home for our children; we
know that our call and our privilege is to provide for the
future. The golden cord, if it exists at all, ties women
and children. The situation cries out for our attention
and our creativity.

Elsewhere, beyond our national borders, in Guate-
mala, for example, homeless children are being killed.
Their crime? They steal food to live. The same is happening to the children of Brazil. The children of the
streets, masses of them, are "a problem," and problems
are to be solved, quickly and expeditiously. If it were not
for Amnesty International, no one would notice.

Furthermore, according to UNICEF, every day
40,000 young children throughout the world die of
other causes, preventable deaths, which would cost little
to prevent. They die from lack of immunization, antibi-
otics and parent education.

In our own country, the number of children in poverty is increasing. In 1988 one in five American children
lived in poverty, 12 million in all. In addition, help for
families struggling against poverty is shrinking. Infant
mortality is very high; the United States ranks 21st
among industrialized nations in this matter.[70] And then

there are issues of children's inner lives. Harvard psychologist and researcher, Robert Coles, together with other researchers, has analyzed responses from over 5,000 children and youth in public, private and parochial schools, in order to explore the range of children's beliefs and moral values and the consequences in their lives. The study is an important one for anyone concerned about both children and the common good.

We learn that children get their moral bearings from a variety of sources, but only 16 percent of the sources are religious. We learn that adults are decisive influences in children's lives: parents, extended family, other adults in the community, especially religious leaders and youth workers, but not all children have caring adults in their lives. We learn that children and youth are worried about harmful behavior, abuse of all kinds, and peer pressure regarding sexual behavior. Still, one reads in this report the hope that children have, even children who live in difficult circumstances. One sees that the light of God's spirit in them is truly inextinguishable.

That divine light is evident in other ways. On September 29, 1990, the United Nations successfully convened more than sixty world leaders to a World Summit for Children. Much of the credit for this historic conference, held in New York City at UN headquarters on September 29, 1990, goes to Mr. James Grant, the executive director of UNICEF. The world leaders were informed of the situation and asked to reverse their usual position of children having the last call on the world's resources. In any civilized society, the leaders were told, children would have the first call. It is too soon to say if the conference was really more about rhetoric than reform, but at the very least the gathering raised the profile of children for all to see. Furthermore, a treaty has been passed by the United Nations, the Convention on the Rights of the Child, which now must be passed by the UN member nations. The United States government, sadly, has made little effort to ratify.

In preparation for the summit of world leaders, the World Conference on Peace and Religion gathered at Princeton Seminary one hundred religious and spiritual leaders to pray together, reason together, and pledge themselves to raise the cause of children with their religious bodies. Shintos, Hindus, Buddhists, Moslems, Christians, Jews all agreed that the principle of the "first call" for children needs to be given life, and that is what our various church bodies should be about. But competing agendas and priorities within religious bodies may mute the urgency.

But in our new home, the home created by women, the home built from those who have known what a "last call" is like, we can commit to the children, those who are born as well as those unborn. We can refuse to bury the cries of the children. We can plead their cause. We can find ways to welcome them home. The possibilities are endless for creative women.

CONCLUSION

The creativity of women is limited only by God's spirit, which we believe is without end. Our structures have channeled this abundant spirit, and the artistic legacy is everywhere. It is in institutions of higher education, like Saint Mary's College. It is in hospitals and school systems. It is in people.

If we were to ask the women who have peopled this lecture to serve as architects for this new home they might advise us to provide for solitude so the spirit can stretch (Sor Juana); and to welcome a vast variety of missions (Mother Austin Carroll); Jane Addams would remind us that the first building erected at Hull House was an art gallery. The quilters would agree that the arts are not only expressive of the soul but of the community. Mothers of families would ask for attention to detail. Feminist theologians would hope that we never cease exploring the hallways of sacred speculation. All would remind us that our history is part of this new home's construction, and that history includes the painful side of our individual and corporate narratives as well as the creative joy. We are building on a foundation nourished by spirit and bone. As Jessica Powers knows that she owes much to her "House of the Silver Spirit," so do we; with her we can say:

Therefore, my music, you must never be
fragile and sweet and a profanity;
Let all my tones be clear and sharp and wild.
This old house bore me in her frosty womb . . .

And some day, others will look about this new home we
erect ". . . faces lifted up to see/this strange new miracle that came to be."[71] And they will be glad.

NOTES

1. Czeslaw Milosz, *Unattainable Earth,* (New York: Ecco Press, 1986).
2. Sr. Madeleva believed that Van Doren was referring to Edna St. Vincent Millay's book, *A Few Figs from Thistles,* quoted in an essay, "Where Are You Going My Pretty Maid?" in *Chaucer's Nuns and Other Essays* by Sr. Madeleva (Port Washington, N.Y.: Kennekot Press, Inc., 1925).
3. Rollo May, *The Courage to Create* (New York: W.W. Norton & Co., 1975), p. 13.
4. Loren Eiseley, *The Night Country* (New York: Charles Scribner's Sons, 1971), pp. 137–138.
5. May, *The Courage to Create,* pp. 32–33.
6. Ibid., p. 44.
7. Ibid., p. 56.
8. George Steiner, *Real Presences* (Chicago: University of Chicago Press, 1989), p. 143.
9. Ibid., p. 147.
10. See Samuel Freedman, *Small Victories* (San Francisco: Harper & Row, 1990) for an inside look at creative teaching in the face of New York City's mega school bureaucracy.
11. May, *The Courage to Create,* p. 19.
12. May Sarton, *Writings on Writing* (Orono, Maine: Puckerbrush Press, 1980) p. 40.
13. Irina Ratushinskaya, "To My Unknown Friend" in *Pencil Letter* (London: Bloodaxe Books, 1988), p. 30.
14. May, *The Courage to Create,* p. 24.

15. Ibid., p. 138.
16. See Cecil Woodham-Smith's biography of Florence Nightingale for insights into her sense of vocation. (New York: McGraw Hill, 1951).
17. For a critical and enlightening treatment of the George Eliot and George Henry Lewes relationship, as well as insight into the marriages of other Victorian writers and intellectuals, see Phyllis Rose's *Parallel Lives* (London and New York: Penguin Books, 1988).
18. Mary Ewens, O.P., "Women in the Convent" in *American Catholic Women: A Historical Exploration,* Karen Kennelly, C.S.J., ed. (New York: MacMillan Publishing Co., 1989), p. 17.
19. See the 1989 Madeleva lecture, *Passionate Women: Two Medieval Mystics* by Elizabeth Dryer (New York/Mahwah: Paulist Press).
20. Octavio Paz, *Sor Juana,* trans. Margaret Sayers Peden (Cambridge, Mass.: The Bellknapp Press of Harvard Univ. Press, 1988).
21. Ibid., p. 109.
22. For insights into the relationship between solitude and creativity see May Sarton's *Journal of a Solitude* (New York/London: W.W. Norton & Co., 1973).
23. Paz, *Sor Juana,* p. 136.
24. Sarton, *Writings on Writing,* p. 40.
25. Paz, *Sor Juana,* p. 102.
26. Ibid., p. 304.
27. Ibid., p. 304.
28. Ibid., p. 424.
29. For all of my information about Mother Austin Carroll I am indebted to Mary Ewens' previously cited chapter in *American Catholic Women.*
30. Ewens, "Women in the Convent" in *American Catholic Women,* p. 30.
31. Ibid., p. 28.
32. See Sandra Schneiders' treatment of the renewal of religious life in *New Wineskins* (New York/Mahwah: Paulist Press, 1986).
33. Colleen McDannell, "Catholic Domesticity 1860–1960" in *American Catholic Women* (New York: MacMillan Publishing Co., 1989), p. 48. I am indebted to McDannell's information on Catholic domesticity in trying to frame this question.
34. Quoted from a nineteenth-century article in *The Baltimore Sun,* cited by McDannell, p. 57.
35. McDannell, "Catholic Domesticity," p. 62.

36. I have written about this childhood devotion in a presentation given at the 1990 Evelyn Underhill symposium sponsored by the National Cathedral of Sts. Peter and Paul in Washington, D.C., and how I experienced those saints in my developing prayer life.

37. McDannell, "Catholic Domesticity," p. 67.

38. Ibid., p. 79.

39. Ibid., p. 79.

40. See the 1980 CARA study of Women in Ministry: A Survey of the Experience of Roman Catholic Women in the United States (Washington, D.C., Center for Applied Research in the Apostolate).

41. For a thorough exposition of the role of Quaker women in American life see Margaret Hope Barron, *Mothers of Feminism* (San Francisco: Harper & Row, 1986).

42. Patricia Cooper and Norma Bradley Allen, *The Quilters: Women and Domestic Art, an Oral History* (New York: Doubleday, 1989).

43. Ibid., p. 17.

44. Ibid., p. 20.

45. Ibid., p. 24.

46. Ibid., pp. 24–25.

47. Ibid., p. 107.

48. Ibid., p. 125.

49. Sandi Fox, "Comments from the Quilt" in *Modern Maturity,* August-September 1990, p. 59.

50. Fox, "Comments from the Quilt," p. 60.

51. The National Museum of American History has a new permanent exhibit, "From Parlor to Politics" which gives women major credit for the great reform movements that swept the United States in the early twentieth century.

52. Margaret Tims, *Jane Addams of Hull House* (London: George Allen & Unwin CTD., 1961), p. 46.

53. Ibid., p. 151.

54. Maria Riley, O.P., *Transforming Feminism* (Kansas City: Sheed & Ward, 1990).

55. Ibid., pp. 16–17.

56. Ibid., p. 17.

57. See Carolyn Heilbrun, *Writing a Woman's Life* (New York/London: W.W. Norton, 1988).

58. See the accounts of St. Catherine of Genoa, for example. The most authoritative description of her teaching is in Friedrich Von Hugel's, *The Mystical Element of Religion* (London: J.M. Dent & Sons Ltd. and James Clarke & Co., Ltd., 1961).

59. *Partners in the Mystery of Redemption: A Pastoral Response to Women's Concerns,* was made public in the spring of 1988 for purposes of further consultation prior redrafting. The text is available from the USCC Office of Publishing and Promotion Services, or from *Origins,* CNS, both in Washington, D.C. The second draft, *One in Christ Jesus,* is available from *Origins.*

60. May, *Courage to Create,* p. 49.

61. Dr. Sharon Parks of Weston School of Theology developed the image of "home" in an unpublished paper presented at the Ecumenical Institute of Spirituality in January, 1986.

62. See Mary Jo Weaver, *New Catholic Women* (San Francisco: Harper & Row, 1986) for a thorough discussion of the concept of women in alliance.

63. Marvine Howe, "Women's Group Seeks Environmental Role" in *The New York Times,* Sunday, Oct. 28, 1990.

64. Jessica Powers, "Robin At Dusk" in *Selected Poetry of Jessica Powers,* ed. Regina Siegfried and Robert Morneau (Kansas City: Sheed & Ward, 1989), p. 187.

65. The Earth Works Group, *50 Simple Things You Can Do to Save the Earth* (Berkeley, CA.: Earthworks Press, 1989).

66. Francine du Plessix Grey, "Soviet Women" in *The New Yorker,* Feb. 19, 1990.

67. See *One in Christ Jesus,* available from *Origins,* Catholic News Service.

68. Deborah Tannen, *You Just Don't Understand* (New York: William Morrow and Co., Inc., 1990).

69. Milosz, "My-ness" in *The Collected Poems* (New York: The Ecco Press, 1988), p. 437.

70. *Youth Record,* Sept. 3, 1990, published by the Youth Policy Institute, Washington, D.C.

71. Jessica Powers, "The House of the Silver Spirit" in *Selected Poetry of Jessica Powers,* p. 125.